D1020601

WHAT'S YOUR HOOK?

26 creative ways to make your message stick.

www.kevincarroll.com

What's Your Hook? is available on www.amazon.com and
www.kevincarroll.com

ISBN: 978-0-9819608-8-3

SECOND
AVENUE
PRESS

THANK YOU

It takes a lot more patience, skill and smarts to listen than it does to talk. While I may be pretty good at talking, my wife, Mary, is superb at listening. Thanks, Hon, for all your support.

To my brother, Mike, who has always been willing to provide his astute editing skills to each one of my manuscripts; I appreciate all your help. Someday you may even be compensated.

To my terrific clients, for being open-minded, willing to take smart risk and finding creative ways to add "hooks" to their presentations, meetings and sales calls. You're a pleasure to work with.

PREFACE

The ability to persuade is an essential stepping stone on the path to success. And common sense tells us that anyone who knows how to grab and keep the attention of an audience has the potential to be a powerful persuader. This book will provide you with a variety of creative ways to capture the attention of anyone, anywhere, anytime.

What's Your Hook? is not just for presenters and salespeople. It's for anyone who wants to ensure that their message sticks with their listener. So whether you're a manager running a meeting, an entrepreneur putting together a marketing brochure, a teacher in front of a class, or a coach motivating a team, you'll find ideas in here that you can use over and over.

I use the word "presentation" as a catchall term. Not only does it mean the typical stand in front of the room type of presentation, but it also can mean running a meeting, hosting a conference call, facilitating a workshop, or having a one-on-one conversation as you would in a job interview. In this book, a "presentation" is anytime you're in front of one or more people for the purpose of delivering a message that you want them to remember.

CONTENTS

The Hooks

*"There are no boring topics,
there are only boring speakers."*

Kevin Carroll

INTRODUCTION

I'll never forget the time my oceanography professor said, "If you're ever swimming in shark-infested waters, always swim with a partner. That way if the shark attacks, you'll at least have a 50/50 chance of surviving." That was over thirty years ago and I still remember his wry piece of advice. He knew how to hook his students.

Take a minute to recall one or two of the most memorable presentations or speeches you have ever seen. Who gave the presentation? Why was it so memorable? What did the presenter say or do that made his or her message stick in your mind? What did they do that hooked you?

Advertising (the industry that I worked in for 17 years) is all about finding "The Hook." Well I shouldn't say that exactly. It's also about knowing who you're trying to reach (your target audience) and having a clear message with a specific benefit. The best advertising is advertising where the creative hook is tied directly to the product rather than having the hook be just an attention grabber and nothing more. As a communicator, if you can successfully connect your hook to your main message, then your audience will be much more likely to remember your key point.

Today I make my living as a professional speaker, corporate trainer and presentation consultant. My job is to help my clients prepare for important meetings and come out as winners. I use hooks all the time both on my sales calls and in my workshops because they work. Every time I use a hook, I can see that it captures the other person's attention and gives my point impact. That's why you should be using them, too.

As I see it, there are two reasons why so many people don't use hooks:

1. They've never been taught how.
2. They're worried that the hook won't work and that they'll end up looking silly.

This book will help solve those two issues.

When it's all said and done, what will you get out of reading this book?

- You'll be a clearer communicator and more persuasive.
- You'll enjoy giving presentations more.
- You'll live happily ever after.

Some Things to Keep in Mind...

1. What is a hook anyway? A hook is any creative device that grabs someone's attention. A hook could be: a catchy phrase, a humorous story, an amazing statistic, a memorable demonstration or a thought-provoking question. Here's my rule of thumb: If you find something interesting, it has the potential to be a hook. The key to using a hook is that you'll want to directly tie your hook (your attention grabber) to the message that you're trying to make stick with your audience.

2. What are the benefits of using hooks?
    a. They grab your listener's attention.
    b. They make your message easier to understand. (This is great when you need to talk about intangible concepts like insurance, consulting services, software or the theory of relativity.)
    c. They make your message more memorable.
    d. They make your message more persuasive.

3. What makes a hook work? Given the fact that humans are highly emotional, inquisitive, creative beings, anything that's different, intriguing and that a person can identify with on a gut level, has the potential to grab their attention.

4. How to make it stick. In order to get your point to stick, it all starts with knowing *exactly* what your point is. If you can't concisely state you key message in one sentence or less, then you're not ready to develop your hook. Remember, the listener shouldn't have to *decipher* your information; their job should be to *absorb* it. That's not to say that they have to agree with you, but they shouldn't sit there wondering what it is you're trying to say.

Here're some examples of focused key points:
- Our goal is to lower our turnover rate from 15% to 8%.
- We want to start a diversity training program.
- We will be moving our operations facility to Peoria.
- We should strive to have 95% of our students graduate.
- We need to increase membership by 5% a year.
- We must increase customer satisfaction ratings from 4.3 to 4.7 in three months.

5. Determine what's in it for them? Not only do you need to be crystal clear on your points, you also need to answer this question: "Why should my audience care?" (What's in it for them?) If the point you're trying to make doesn't affect them directly, or doesn't provide any value to them, then they'll filter you out. You need to show them exactly how you are going to either increase their pleasure or decrease their pain. (This is your *value proposition.*) Here are some samples:
- Make more money
- Have less stress
- Gain more respect
- Have less homework

- Increase visibility
- Save on repairs
- Improve productivity

6. Your message needs to be clear, concise and well organized. To that end, if you need help with how to plan your presentation or your message, I suggest you read my first book: *Make Your Point!*. That book is an excellent complement to this book. It delves into the important strategic questions you should ask yourself such as: Who's my audience? What's my objective? What's in it for them? It also provides the reader with a template I call *The Diamond* which provides the reader with a tool for organizing almost any presentation. *Make Your Point!* is the steak and *What's Your Hook?* is the sizzle. Both are important.

7. Start a *Keeper Folder*. A keeper folder is simply a manila folder marked with the word "KEEPERS" big and bold on the outside. Anytime you come across something that grabs your attention and that you find interesting (it could be a newspaper or magazine article, a photo, a quote, a surprising statistic, or whatever) put it in your keeper folder. That way, the next time you have to communicate an important message and you're looking for some hooks, you'll already have some in your keeper folder. Along the same lines, when someone tells you to check out an amazing website (like coolsiteoftheday.com) or they email you something funny, save it in an electronic version of your keeper folder. That will give you another handy resource when it comes time to find a hook.

8. Create a story file. Start writing down your great stories and anecdotes; both the ones from your past as well as the ones that are yet to come. A story could be about the time you backed your dad's car into your mom's car. It could be about a stranger who said a kind word to you when you needed it most, or when you got a hole in one. As you'll see in the chapter called *Personal Stories,* a story is nothing more than an incident that happened to you that's funny, frightening, inspiring or unusual. Let me repeat that since I hear people sometimes moan, "But I don't have any stories." A story is nothing more than an incident that happened to you that's funny, frightening, inspiring or unusual. Stories can be as brief as 10 seconds or as long as 5 minutes (although it better be a real good one if it's 5 minutes). Start writing down your stories now so that when you need them, you have them.

9. Consider this book a reference tool. Take what you need and leave the rest. Even if you only take away three or four ideas, the key is to PUT THEM TO USE! Test the waters; discover which hooks work best for you. Focus on the ones you believe will give you the best return. Once you've tried using a few, come back and read the book again. You'll have a different perspective on it the second time around.

So to recap...
- First, be absolutely clear on your point(s).
- Second, know what's in it for your audience.
- Third, find a hook(s) that will help make your point(s) stick.

"It usually takes more than three weeks to prepare a good impromptu speech."

Mark Twain

The
HOOKS

PERSONAL STORIES

Of all the different, creative ways to hook an audience, personal stories are my favorite. A personal story is where you take an incident from your own life and you *draw a parallel* between that incident and the point you're trying to make in your presentation. Personal stories are an emotional hook and, when done right, are magic. Audiences understand them, they relate to them and they remember them. This, in turn, helps them remember your point.

Stories, when used in presentations, meetings and conversations, are most effective when you apply this three-step process:

1. Tell your story. The best stories are *specific moments* in time where something happened that was either funny, frightening, inspiring or unusual.

2. Make just *one* point. For example, you might say: "What I discovered that day was that it's really important to get outside your comfort zone. Or "That experience helped me realize that there are different ways to accomplish the same objective." Don't make more than *one* point, otherwise it will dilute your message.

3. Make the point relevant to your listeners. This is where you make a connection between the point you just made and how it relates to your audience.

A few years ago I was running a workshop with a team of financial advisors and I was teaching them my three-part storytelling process. One of the participants then volunteered to give it a try. Here's the story he told to his fellow advisors:

I moved to Colorado from Brazil when I was 16 years old and I didn't speak a word of English. (Great stories have conflict or difficulty at their core.) *Well the good news was that I started dating a girl in my high school soon after I moved to the United States. As it turned out, this girl happened to live on a ranch.*

One day I called her at her home and I meant to ask her, "Do you have any horses?" But what I said was, "You remind me of a horse." He then shook his head and said, *"Well that was the end of that relationship."* With that, all the financial advisors laughed. The presenter went on to say, *"What I realized that day was that it's really important to speak the same language as the people you're with. In our jobs as financial advisors, we often talk about things like return on investment, portfolio analysis and debt/equity ratios, but our clients speak*

a different language than we do. They want to know:
Can I retire in 10 years? Can I pay for college for my
kid? Can I afford to take a vacation? So it's critical
that we speak our client's language and not our lan-
guage. And if we do, we'll be a lot more successful.

That's a perfect execution of how to use personal stories in
a business presentation.

This next story was told to me by a beverage salesman in
one of my seminars. He uses it to teach other salespeople
how to be more successful:

When I went to buy my first car, I didn't have very
much money, so I asked the salesperson to show
me his least expensive model. I took one look at the
price and I knew I couldn't afford it. I then asked him
if he had the same car, but with no extra features.
Well the second car he showed me had a lower
sticker price, but I still couldn't afford it. So I asked if
he had anything that was even cheaper. We then
went out back and he showed me a car I could
actually afford. I asked him why it was less expensive
than the car we had just seen in the showroom and
he told me that the other car was an automatic and
that this one was a standard. I said that I didn't know
how to drive a standard so I couldn't buy the car. He
then responded, "Why don't you get in the passen-
ger seat and we'll take it for a drive just so you can

> see how it feels." Two minutes into the test drive the
> salesperson drove the car up a steep hill, stopped it
> half way, put the parking break on and got out of
> the car. He walked around to my side and said, "I'm
> going to teach you how to drive it." He then spent
> over an hour with me until I mastered it. When we got
> back to the showroom, I bought the car. That day I
> saw firsthand what it really meant to go above and
> beyond a customer's expectations. It was one of the
> best sales lessons I've ever learned and I encourage
> you, as salespeople, to look at customer resistance
> as an opportunity to help them out.

By the way, audiences love it when we poke good-natured
fun at ourselves rather than when we are the hero of our
own story. Here's a personal story I sometimes tell in my
Breakthrough Thinking seminar just to loosen up the participants.

> A number of years ago, while working at an advertis-
> ing agency, I was talking with one of the guys
> who handled a camera account. I asked
> him if he was working on anything
> new and he told me that his cli-
> ent was involved in a whole new
> type of photography called
> digital photography. He said
> that there would come a day in
> the not too distant future where

people wouldn't use film in their cameras. Well I didn't know what he was talking about because I couldn't get my head around the concept that cameras wouldn't use film. In fact, I thought that the whole idea sounded like a waste of time. As I walked away I sort of snickered and said "Well good luck with that project."

This story always gets a laugh and sets the tone that the class will be fun and that no one has all the answers.

If you want to be a great storyteller (and who doesn't?) you have to start writing down your stories. Think back on those incidences in your life that were funny, frightening, inspiring or unusual. It could have been the time you got your first speeding ticket, or the day you witnessed a bank holdup, or the time a glob of roofing tar landed on you right before an important meeting. (Welcome to my world.) If you jot down these past incidences and add new ones as they come along, you'll have instant access to a bunch of rich stories and anecdotes whenever you need one. As I mentioned, it's MUCH easier to have a collection of great stories at the ready then to have to come up with a story the night before a presentation.

When I log my stories, I jot down two or three key ideas within the story. This makes it easy to find the most appropriate stories whether I'm talking about communication, persistence, listening, effective selling techniques, honesty, or whatever.

ANALOGIES

Analogies are wonderful because listeners can easily identify with them, they help make vague concepts more concrete and they can add some zing to your message. Read the front page of any major newspaper in America and you're sure to find at least one analogy. In fact, the next time you pick up a newspaper or magazine, take a look at a few articles and you'll discover how frequently writers use analogies to help get their point across.

Strong speakers use analogies in many different ways. They can be used as a quick hit to immediately capture a point, or a speaker might even build an entire presentation around one analogy that has many facets. A recent example of a quick-hit is when Representative Barney Frank, who is openly gay, once said during a hearing: "People aren't good at doing things they dislike. It's like asking me to judge the Miss America contest - if your heart's not in it, you don't do a very good job."

A computer engineer once needed to communicate to a non-IT person that having three different software platforms was a bad idea. He used this analogy:

Having three different platforms is a lot like having three different brands of air conditioners in your home. Every time you need to replace the filters, you have to go through the hassle of finding three different types. That may even mean going to three different stores. And every time one of your air conditioners has to be repaired, you might have to contact a different manufacturer. It just doesn't make sense.

When I work with clients I ask them to come up with an interesting analogy for what their job is like. I specifically tell them that they can't use "fireman" as their analogy because there's nothing unique or memorable about saying, "My job's a lot like being a fireman." I also tell them that they can't say, "My job is a lot like being a consultant." Why not? Because "consultant" is vague and doesn't help clarify what your job is. It's also a boring analogy and therefore won't be very memorable. Here are a couple of attention-grabbing analogies I've heard my clients use to describe their jobs:

*My job is a lot like being a **UN weapons inspector.** I have to go into places where I'm not welcomed and find information that no one wants to give me.*

*My job is a lot like being a **gold miner.** I have to find nuggets of valuable* *information buried under lots of unimportant data.*

Try this exercise: Come up with an interesting and unique analogy for your own job:

> *My job is a lot like being a*_____.

> *I have to*_____.

Is it specific?   Is it unique?   Is it memorable?

Here's a couple more analogies. Can you see how they make otherwise dull concepts come alive?

- "MTV is to music as KFC is to chicken." (Lewis Black)
- "Pupils are more like oysters than sausages. The job of teaching is not to stuff them and then seal them up, but to help them open and reveal the riches within. There are pearls in each of us, if only we knew how to cultivate them with ardor and persistence." (Sydney J. Harris)

Since we're talking about analogies, I thought you'd get a kick out of some of the *worst* analogies written in a high school essay. (As bad as they are, they're pretty funny.)

- The plan was simple, like my brother-in-law Phil. But un-like Phil, this plan just might work.
- The little boat gently drifted across the pond exactly

the way a bowling ball wouldn't.

- From the attic came an unearthly howl. The whole scene had an eerie, surreal quality, like when you're on vacation in another city and *Jeopardy* comes on at 7 p.m. instead of 7:30.

- Her eyes were like two brown circles with big black dots in the center.

- His thoughts tumbled in his head, making and breaking alliances like underpants in a dryer without Cling Free.

- He was as tall as a six-foot-three-inch tree.

- The politician was gone but unnoticed, like the period after the Dr. on a Dr Pepper can.

- John and Mary had never met. They were like two hummingbirds who had also never met.

*"Creativity comes from trust.
Trust your instincts."*

Rita Mae Brown

EXAMPLES

Examples are real world illustrations of ideas or concepts. Examples have tremendous value to presenters and salespeople, because they solidify intangible concepts or ideas. The more specific and concrete your examples are, the more effective they will be in helping you get your points across. Without them, your audience will wonder, "What's he talking about?" Examples are mandatory whether you're giving a presentation or conversing one-on-one as you would in a job interview. Although examples may lack some of the wow factor that other types of hooks have, that doesn't diminish their importance. Examples help listeners "get it."

I remember coaching a woman who had terrific delivery skills and a well-organized message. What was strange about her presentation was that even though she had great skills, I couldn't quite figure out what she was talking about nor could I remember much of what he had just said when she was finished. I then realized what the problem

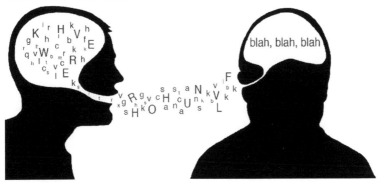

was. She had no examples to help illuminate her points. Her ideas stayed on an abstract, conceptual level and were difficult to grasp. Once she added a few examples, then her message had total clarity.

I can say to my kids, "It's important for you to work as a team." But that's vague. Clarity comes when I add, "For example, Claire, if you don't have the time to clear your plate because you have to run off to a softball game, then Collin please clear it for her." Similarly, I can give a pitch to a prospect and tell him "I can help you make your presentations more persuasive and memorable," but unless I tell him about the time I once had a presenter hand out a thousand bags of M&M's in order to get a thousand audience members to remember the words "**M**ind share to **M**arket share" then my prospect won't really understand how I make presentations more memorable. (I'll go in to more detail about this example in the chapter on PROPS.)

So whenever or wherever you're communicating, make certain you lace your message with clear, crisp examples so that those on the receiving end truly understand what you're talking about. You'll find that when you provide your listeners with good examples, that's when you'll see their heads nod indicating that you're getting your point across.

QUESTIONS

The easiest way to get your audience involved is by asking them a question. I'm a big believer that presentations (and certainly sales calls) should be more like conversations and less like monologues. If communication is about the transfer of ideas from one person to another, then you want that to be a two-way process to help ensure that the message is being received. Questions can do that for you.

So why don't presenters create more of a dialogue by asking questions? Well, in my opinion, they're afraid because they...

- Don't see other presenters doing it.
- Want to avoid being challenged by an audience member.
- Believe that they might lose control and the audience could take them "off message."
- Think that the audience will just sit there and not say anything.

While I have empathy for those of you that have these fears, if you go about asking questions the right way, you'll see that your concerns can be greatly diminished.

Speaking of fear, keep in mind that, as a presenter, your perception of time is much different than your audience's. When you ask your audience a question, you're going to feel some anxiousness if you don't get a response instantaneously. However, you have to remember that your audience needs time to process your question and time to formulate their answer before they open their mouths. I learned this the hard way when I tried standup comedy many years ago. When I hit my first punch line I didn't give the audience enough time to process the joke. So I mistakenly started my next joke just as they began laughing at the first one. Then, unfortunately, they couldn't hear the set-up for my second joke because they were laughing at the first one. This messed up my timing for the rest of my routine and it turned into the longest ten minutes of my life.

To repeat myself, when you ask your audience a question, expect them to take a little time to process the question and come up with an answer. Too often speakers panic if they don't hear a response in six nanoseconds. I once witnessed a very senior executive ask a question to an audience of over 1,000. When no one answered instantly, she overreacted and said "Is anybody out there paying attention?" All that did was alienate her audience.

If your audience doesn't respond within seven to ten seconds, either they didn't understand the question or they need a little more time to process it. When that happens, I usually rephrase or restate the question. I once asked this convoluted question to a large audience: "What are some of the interpersonal communication challenges you face?" Ugh. No one gave an answer because that's a vague question. The next time I tried it I simplified it to: "What do people do that ticks you off?" I got lots of responses to that question.

Another approach is to give your audience a heads-up a few minutes before you ask them a question. You simply say, "In a minute I'd like to get your opinion on such and such." This helps them get their antennae up before you ask the actual question.

Audience participation has a lot going for it. First, it makes the presenter look more like they're in control because, paradoxically, they're willing to give up some control. Second, it makes for a much more interesting and lively presentation. Third, it helps ensure that the presenter's message is being absorbed. And fourth, it takes off some of the pressure that's on the presenter. With that said, I realize that many times the situation mandates that the presenter just stand up, give their spiel and not ask the audience questions. Fine, but try to make that the exception rather than the rule.

Keep in mind that when you ask your audience a question, ask open-ended, interesting questions. Rather than saying, "How many people want to make more money?" Try this instead: "If you won $100,000 in the lottery, how would you spend it?" That's a more intriguing question.

Here are some of the questions I usually ask right at the beginning of my workshops:
- On a scale of 1 to 10, how are you feeling about being here today? Why?
- What are some of the biggest challenges you face on your job?
- What do you like most about your job? Least?
- What would make today a homerun for you?

Incidentally, I think it's very powerful to ask questions right at the start of your meeting or presentation (even if they're rhetorical questions.) By doing this, you take the pressure off of you, you engage your listeners, and you set the tone for a give and take of information.

EYE-CATCHING VISUALS

Imagine turning on the news and rather than seeing the anchorperson front and center, he or she was off to the side, in the shadows, reading bullet points as you, the viewer, read along with them. That would look pretty lame. Yet that's what goes on in countless conference rooms every day. Presenters walk to the front of the room, they stand to the side of the conference table, the lights are lowered, and then lots of words and numbers fill the screen. Is this really the best way to communicate? (The correct answer would be "No.")

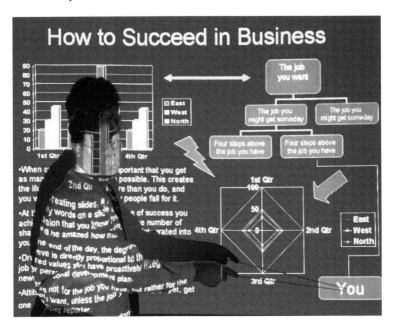

Humans are *visual* creatures. The best communicators know this and they leverage *visual images* to get their points across. Very simply, presentations should have fewer words, fewer numbers, and more pictures. Your goal should be to identify the key concepts you are trying to communicate and let images (photos and illustrations) capture those ideas. The words and data you show on screen should be limited to just the information that matters. Does your audience really need to see the 5-year, 52-week trend of your 32 oz. pomegranate juice in Des Moines?

Don't you just love the horrific slide shown on the previous page? How often have you seen visuals like this one? Probably plenty of times. The slide is crammed with too much info, the color scheme is lousy, the font is way too small and it's confusing. Not to mention the nifty way the presenter has integrated himself right into the slide. It looks like he's wearing PowerPoint camouflage. The other slides shown here are

much more effective because they have a big, bold image and they emphasize one major point followed by 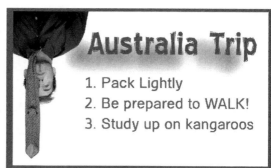 supporting points.

Benefits of Recycling

Reduce expenses 7.5%
Tax incentives
Green certification

I like slides like these because they help rein-force the main point the pre-senter is trying to make, they're engaging, and they aren't over-loaded with too much information. (Save your details for your backup slides or, better yet, a handout.)

I'm not suggesting that all your slides should look like these three. It's perfectly fine having some slides that have num-bers, tables, charts and graphs, but, fundamentally, I'd recommend that you back off on doing a data dump and work in more graphics in order to help communicate your message.

$ales Contest

Northwest Region
1st and 2nd Quarters
Specialty Brands Only

You can easily download inexpensive, high-quality pho-tos like the ones you see above from stock photography companies like www.istockphoto.com, www.iClipart.com or www.shutterstock.com. With just a basic understanding of PowerPoint, you can overlay words onto the pictures. For another great resource, go to: www.presentationzen.com. There you'll find plenty of examples of top-notch slides.

So here's your challenge. For your next pitch, pull back on the words and numbers and add more pictures. You'll be glad you did.

PROPS

Here are six great reasons why you should use props in your next presentation or on a sales call.

1. Props make abstract ideas more concrete.
2. Props make mundane content more interesting.
3. Props give you, the presenter, a way to stand out.
4. Props are easy to incorporate into any message.
5. Props connect you to your listener(s).
6. Props are limitless.

Props are simply any three dimensional object that a presenter uses during a presentation to help illustrate a point. Props could include just about anything: a newspaper, a hammer, a mouse (computer or otherwise), a plant, a beach ball, a glass of water, a hose, an air filter, a mirror, a whip (let's not go there), a stuffed animal, a pumpkin... A prop is *anything* that you can connect to your message either directly or indirectly. Props, because they're tangible, add visual anchors to verbal concepts.

Here are a few clever examples of how some of my clients have used props:
The CEO of a software company had an ongoing prob-

lem. Some of his customers were receiving his company's software without all of the instructions. He had talked to his team about the issue, but it was still happening. He then called me because he wasn't sure why his message wasn't sticking. I told him that I had good news and bad news. The good news was that I clearly understood what he was trying to communicate. (It surprises me how often people aren't even sure what their point is.) But I also told him that the bad news was that he didn't have a hook, so therefore it would be pretty tough to get his message to sink in. After I cited a few examples of what I meant by a hook, I could see that he totally understood how powerful hooks can be. He told me he'd try to find just the right hook. Two weeks later the CEO called me and shared this story:

As usual, I got everybody together for our Monday morning staff meeting and I opened by saying, "Before we get started, I wanted to kick off our meeting with a little friendly competition so I went to the bank this weekend and took out three, $100 bills. (He held them up for all to see.) I also went out and bought identical puzzles for everyone in the room." (He then handed out little plastic puzzles that were each inside a pouch.) *I told my staff, "On the count of three, open your pouch and solve your puzzle as quickly as you can. As soon* *as you put it together, run up here and if you're one of the first three people to finish, you'll win $100." I then counted to three and everybody immediately ripped into their puzzles and started working on them. After just a minute or so, one person yelled, "I got it!" and ran up and collected their reward. Moments later two others ran up and grabbed their money as well. With that, everyone around the conference table let out a big groan. One employee turned to one of the winners and asked, 'How'd you do it so quickly?' The winner said, "It was easy. I just read the instructions." Then the other two winners concurred, "Yeah, we just read the instructions." Well, with that, the room erupted. The losers started to complain and needled me about the fact that the winners had received the instructions and they hadn't. They said the game wasn't fair and they looked miffed. I just stood there and listened. When the moaning died down I said, "Now you know how our customers feel when they get our software and they don't receive all the information they need...it's just not fair."*

This is an outstanding example that shows the power of the hook. It's simple, emotional (feeling cheated is very emotional) and is directly connected to the point that the presenter wanted to make.

Let me repeat what I've been saying all along...The core to finding a great hook is to first, be absolutely clear about what your point is and then second, find something that makes the same point, but in an entirely different way. If you can do this, you'll be a world class hooker. (So to speak.)

Here are some more examples:

Another client of mine, who worked for a prestigious insurance company, recounted how she recently used props to convince the owner of an upscale bakery to buy insurance from her. Having met with the prospect on a previous occasion, she knew that his concern about buying insurance from her had to do with the cost. From his perspective, he felt that all insurance was pretty much the same, so why should he buy it

"Creativity is the power to connect the seemingly unconnected."

William Plomer

from her and pay more for it? Her challenge, therefore, was to convince the baker why her insurance coverage, although more expensive than her competitors', was well worth it.

When she sat down with the prospect, she pulled out two loaves of bread and put them on the table in front of her.

She casually said, "Before we get started, maybe you can help me understand something. This morning I went to the supermarket and bought a fresh loaf of bread and then when I arrived here I bought a loaf of your bread. You  know, they look pretty much identical, but your bread is much more expensive. I was wondering what makes your bread so special? With that, the baker jumped in and enthusiastically explained why his bread was so much better than the supermarket loaf. He talked about the ingredients, the recipe, how it was baked and, of course, the taste. After he was finished, the insurance saleswoman thanked him for helping her understand the differences between the two loaves and she then segued into her pitch by saying, "Well I guess your bread is a lot like our insurance. On the surface it looks like any other type of coverage, but if you look at it more closely..."

Guess what? She got the business.

The marketing director for a small South American winery had the difficult task of trying to gain the attention of the distributor sales force. At the end of his presentation he took off his jacket, tie and shirt and revealed an Argentinean polo shirt with the number 4 on it and said, "I know that you have three major wine brands that you'll be focusing on this season. All I'm asking for is that you carve out a little time when you're calling on retailers and make my wine brand your *fourth* priority." The visual of him in the polo shirt with the number 4 on it was much more powerful than if he simply talked about it.

Jack Mitchell, the owner of a very successful men's clothing store in Westport, Connecticut wrote a book called *Hug Your Customer*. The book became a big success and Jack was subsequently asked to speak before numerous audiences. At the beginning of all his speeches he would unravel a yellow measuring tape (a tailor's tape) and drape it around his neck. It was a catchy little prop that set the tone that he was just an average guy and that his presentation was going to be casual and relaxed.

The last example I'll give you of the successful use of props comes from an experience I had while coaching a very senior executive at a leading technology company. Two weeks before she had to present to a thousand salespeople from around the globe, she asked me to sit down with her and her speechwriter. After seeing her presentation, which was jam-packed with information, I asked, "What's the one thing you want your salespeople to remember?" She said, "I want my team to turn mind-share into market-share." So I asked, "If I can get your team to remember mind-share to market-share, you'll be happy." "Absolutely" she replied. With that, her speechwriter said, "Well hold on a minute. In one breath you're telling us that there's too much information in the presentation and in the next breath you're telling us we have to add some of your fluff." "Fluff!?" I yelped. "This fluff is the thing that's going to make the presentation memorable." I guess that did the trick because we then went on to brainstorm different types of hooks such as stories, anecdotes, analogies and whatnot. Our goal was to find a creative way to get the audience to remember mind-share to market-share. After a few minutes the speechwriter said, "Well mind-share to market-share is alliteration. It's M & M." I then announced, "Guess what? We have our hook."

Two weeks later, a thousand salespeople walked into the hotel ballroom, sat down and they each had a bag of M&M's in front of them. The executive kicked off the three-day meeting by saying, "Before I get started, you should know that the bag of M&M's you have in front of you has something to do with my presentation and the first person to guess what that connection is, will win a prize from me. I then heard a strange noise. It was the crinkling sound of a thousand bags of M&M's being picked up, looked at, opened and eaten (the M&M's, not the bags). So here it was, less than a minute into her presentation and she had the entire audience totally engaged. About 40 minutes into her presentation, she began talking about e-business and mind-share to market-share. Someone yelled out "M&M's" and when he got up on stage to collect his prize, he was awarded a humongous bag of M&M's. The audience laughed and the point was made. Oh yeah, on their last night at the hotel, the salespeople did not get a chocolate mint on their pillow. They got a mini bag of M&M's with a note from the executive thanking them for their efforts.

What prop can you use in your very next presentation, meeting or sales call?

"The whole object of comedy is to be yourself and the closer you get to that, the funnier you will be."

Jerry Seinfeld

SURPRISING STATISTICS

Each day millions of innocent people sit in meetings and get buried alive in facts and figures. This tragedy can be prevented and you can help. (Sounds like a white collar public service announcement, doesn't it?)

While numbers, facts and figures are important because they can be used to communicate pertinent information and to support your points, numbers can be overdone. Rather than dumping mounds of mundane stats on your audience, you're better off cutting back on the numbing numbers and instead find fascinating facts. In other words, you need surprising statistics. Surprising statistics make great hooks because they grab the left brain of your listener and give it a good shake.

The key word here is *surprising*. Your goal should be to present your data so that it's both interesting and provocative. Your aim is to grab your audience's attention (or in the case of email, your reader's attention) and get them to remember what you said. For example, in the August 17th 1998 issue of *The New Yorker*, the writer wanted to convey that the American public had unrealistically high expectations for their mutual funds, he wrote: *The typical mutual fund investor expects annual returns from the stock market of thirty-four percent over the next ten years - which implies that the Dow will be about 136,500 in 2008.*

That's much better than simply saying: *The typical mutual fund investor expects annual returns from the stock market of thirty-four percent over the next ten years.*

Here are a few more surprising statistics:

This was on the *Forbes* website and it was used to communicate the awesome processing power of a network switch that Cisco Systems was working on:

On Monday, Cisco announced the development of the Nexus 7000, a network switch that's capable of routing 15 terabits of data per second--the equivalent of moving the entire contents of Wikipedia in a hundredth of a second, or downloading every movie available on Netflix in about 40 seconds.

Had the reporter stopped at "15 terabits of data per second" that would get a big yawn from the reader.

A reporter for *The Washington Post* once used a series of surprising statistics to help make a case for investing in equities over fixed income assets such as bonds, because equities yield higher returns over time. Here's what he wrote:

• Let's take Peter Minuit's purchase of Manhattan

from the Indians in 1626 for $24 worth of trinkets. Compounded at 6 percent annually (an aggressive bond rate), that $24 would be worth $78 billion today. Compounded at 10% annually (slightly below the average stock return), $24 would become $87 trillion.

- If you had invested $1,000 in a basket of large company stocks in 1926, you would have $2,279,000 by the end of 2001. The same amount invested in bonds would have grown to just $51,000; in Treasury bills, to $17,000.

This surprising fact was excerpted from *The Tipping Point* by Malcolm Gladwell:

Among the general population, about 14.5% of all men are 6 feet or taller. If you look at CEO's of Fortune 500 companies, 58% are over 6 feet. Over the course of a lifetime, the average man who is 6'5" will make hundreds of thousands of dollars more than someone who is 5' 9".

I once saw this startling statistic which was intended to put the number of deaths caused in plane crashes into perspective: "More people are killed by donkeys in a year than die in plane crashes." Granted, it's a bizarre stat, but it might help diminish one's concern when it comes to boarding a jet. (I wonder if anyone has ever researched how many donkeys are killed in plane crashes every year...hmmm.)

Here are some statistics from 1905. These surprising stats could be used to talk about change, technology, the past, the future...

- The average life expectancy in the U.S. was 47 years.
- Only 14 percent of the homes in the U.S. had a bathtub.
- Only 8 percent of the homes had a telephone.
- A three-minute call from Denver to New York City cost eleven dollars.
- There were only 8,000 cars in the U.S., and only 144 miles of paved roads.
- The maximum speed limit in most cities was 10 mph.
- The average wage in the U.S. was 22 cents per hour.
- The average U.S. worker made between $200 and $400 per year.
- Most women washed their hair once a month.

While it's great to find surprising statistics that are directly related to your topic, you can often find some amazing numbers that are indirectly related and they can work just as well. One of my clients opened her presentation by asking everyone in the meeting to write down how long they thought it took to build the Empire State Building? (What would you guess?) She concluded her presentation by saying, "Given that it took only thirteen months to build the Empire State Building, I'm confident that we can complete Project X in half that time."

Keep in mind that surprising statistics don't do you any good unless you use them to help make your point stick. Don't use surprising statistics just for the sake of using them.

HUMOR

Many people mistakenly believe that "humor" means the same thing as "tell jokes." While joke-telling is a form of humor, there are lots of other types of humor that can work just as well (if not better) and that you can feel more comfortable with. The list includes: funny newspaper articles, humorous trivia questions, amusing bumper stickers, cartoons, outlandish photos, top ten lists, embarrassing moments, entertaining anecdotes and (if all else fails) puns. There are three criteria I apply when deciding whether or not to use humor in a presentation.

1. Is it funny? (Brilliant criteria, isn't it?)
2. Is it in good taste?
3. Does it relate to the topic I'm talking about?

Keep in mind that rather than trying to be "funny," you're better off just trying to add some 'fun' into your presentation. It's a lot easier making something fun rather than trying to be funny. (See the chapter on GAMES for ways to add fun.)

Here's a short list of some humorous things I've either incorporated or thought about incorporating into presentations to add levity. I didn't come up with these ditties myself. They were either sent to me or I found them on the internet. As you come across funny witticisms similar to the ones you see below, save them in your KEEPERS file so that you can pull them out whenever you need them. They're perfect for sales meetings, brand reviews, conferences, team meetings, and project kickoffs.

Mock Motivational Quotes
- "Before you criticize someone, you should walk a mile in their shoes. That way, when you criticize them, you're a mile away and you have their shoes."
- "Always remember you're unique, just like everyone else."
- "He who smiles in a crisis has found someone to blame."

Strange Product Instructions
- On a package for an iron: "Do not iron clothes on body."
- On Nytol Sleep Aid: "Warning: May cause drowsiness".
- On a box of Christmas lights: "For indoor or outdoor use only".

Funny Bumper Stickers
- 43% of statistics are useless.
- He who laughs last, thinks slowest.
- Iliterate? Write for help.

How to Deal with Telemarketers
- Insist that the caller is really your buddy, Carl, playing a joke: "Come on, Carl, cut it out! Seriously, Carl, how's your momma?"
- If they start out with, "How are you today?" say, "I'm so glad you asked, because no one these days seems to care, and I have all these problems. My arthritis is acting up, my eyeballs are sore, my dog just threw up, I just found the chicken cutlet that I dropped behind the stove last year..."
- If they say they're John Doe from XYZ Company, ask them to spell their name. Then ask them to spell the company name. Then ask them where it is located, how long it has been in business, how many people work there, how they got into this line of work, if they are married, how many kids they have, etc. Continue asking them personal questions or questions about their company for as long as necessary.

Things not to say in a Job Interview: (from Radaronline.com)

- "Hope you don't mind, but I brought my own chair."
- "If I smell like Cheez-Its, it's just because I love them so freakin' much."
- "What in the hell is this Microsoft Word everyone's been talking about?"
- "Do you believe in fairies?"
- "Wow. The valium just kicked in."
- "It's not that I prefer to work independently; it always just seems to end up that way."

Actual Statements Made During Court Cases

Judge: I know you, don't I?

Defendant: Uh, yes.

Judge: All right, tell me, how do I know you?

Defendant: Judge, do I have to tell you?

Judge: Of course, you might be obstructing justice not to tell me.

Defendant: Okay. I was your bookie.

From a defendant representing himself...

Defendant: Did you get a good look at me when I stole your purse?

Victim: Yes, I saw you clearly. You are the one who stole my purse.

Defendant: I should have shot you while I had the chance.

Judge: The charge here is theft of frozen chickens. Are you the defendant?

Defendant: No, sir, I'm the guy who stole the chickens.

VIDEO CLIPS

Audiences are so accustomed to seeing video everywhere they look, whether it's on TV, iTunes, the movies, YouTube, or what have you. Because of that, people have become used to being stimulated and engaged through video. The question isn't whether or not I should use video, but rather, what kind of video should I use?

The good news is that it's never been easier to find or create a video segment that can fit your presentation, meeting or sales call. There are video clips available on everything from adjusting a bike derailleur, to workplace safety, to how to raise a happy hamster. (To tell the truth, I'm not sure about the hamster one, but let's go with it.)

No matter what subject you're presenting on, you can either find a video clip that relates directly to your point or you can find one that relates indirectly. Either way, video can be used as a hook. For example, when I teach presentation skills, I often show a video clip of a hotel doorman whom I met in Dallas, Texas. The video is great because it demonstrates how an individual can instantly project both confidence and likeability through non-verbal behaviors. My clients find the video interesting, clarifying and memorable. Similarly, if I was giving a presentation on risk management, I could start off by showing a short, compelling video of a mountain climber. So whether you show a clip that directly connects to your topic or one that is allegorical, try working video into your message. Keep in mind that technology has a way of surprising us, so make sure you have a back-up plan ready just in case your video goes kaput.

So where do you find good video clips? Well, through the marvels of the internet, you should be able to track down some great footage in a half hour or less. Some clips will cost you, others are free. Also, some videos have restrictions as to what you can or can not show in a public forum, so do your homework beforehand. (Go to www.creativecommons.org to get more information on how to find content that is available for public use.)

Here are some terrific sources for video:

YouTube - An endless supply of videos...some remarkable, some not so remarkable. In the future, when you come across a video that grabs you either because it's funny, inspiring, or amazing, try to get in the habit of bookmarking it. Then, the next time you have to do a presentation, look back on your YouTube favorites and see which one(s) you might integrate into your pitch.

Stumbleupon.com, Metacafe.com - If you can't find what you're looking for on YouTube, check these two sites out.

5min.com - Instructional videos on a wide variety of topics. The videos run about three minutes each and because they are submitted by their members, the quality varies. Generally they're really good, so check it out. Yobler.com is another instructional video site.

JibJab.com - This is a commercial site where you can produce (quite easily) goofy videos by uploading photos of people into JibJab's animated videos. *The Dancing Elves* was a smash hit at Christmas a while back. For not too much money, you can produce a very humorous piece that will get your audience chuckling. Let's say you're the principal of a school and you want to have fun with the teachers at an upcoming Teachers' In-service Day, JibJab could come in real handy.

Animoto.com - I'd suggest that you put down this book and go here right away. With Animoto, you can upload your favorite digital photos, press a few buttons and, within minutes, create a high-quality, MTV-style video featuring the photos you just uploaded. I couldn't believe it when I first saw this site. 30-second videos are free. For longer videos you pay just $30 for 12 months of unlimited use. Feel free to use my promotional code (PNTDVLZA) and save $5. (I have no affiliation with the company.)

Here are three ways you might use Animoto:

1. Imagine you're at an office outing and you take a bunch of pictures of your coworkers. Afterwards, you upload the photos into Animoto and at dinner you present the video to the gang. They'll get a kick out of it and you'll get promoted to Senior VP of Morale.

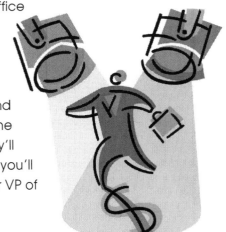

2. You're launching a new product and you're trying to build excitement within your company. At the end of your presentation (which will be highly engaging because you have worked in a number of hooks along the way) you show a high-energy Animoto video of the product and the team that helped launch it.

3. There's a retirement party for Alice in Accounting. You show an Animoto video that celebrates Alice's time at the company. She'll love it.

I found a site called the Educational Technology Clearinghouse which listed a number of video sources including the ones cited below. You'll find some pretty incredible stuff here. Be aware of which videos you are allowed to use and which ones you not allowed to use.

Movie Archive - A moving image archive with 17,478 downloadable video files. Collections include: vintage TV adds, educational, industrial, and amateur videos.

The Library of Congress Motion Picture Collection - Collections of downloadable motion pictures on topics such as the Spanish-American War, Presidential Inaugurations and September 11th.

The Open Video Project - Free, downloadable video from a variety of sources including video programs obtained from U.S. government agencies such as the U.S. Records and Archives Administration and NASA. There are options to select footage in color or black & white, as well as movies with sound or without.

Newsfilm Online - Produced by ITN, the world's largest independent news organization, this website offers a number of ITN news stories available to download for free, arranged by theme and date. Categories include: Art, Black and Asian Issues, Technology, Crime, Crowds, Health, Language, Natural Disasters, Weather, Science, Technology, Fashion, and US Civil Rights.

Lastly, if you can't find a preexisting video from any of the above sources, you can either produce your own or, if you have the budget, have a production house make one for you. Here's an example: One of my clients wanted to use a video clip in his brand presentation at a national sales meeting in front of a thousand people. His goal was to get the audience pumped up and to get them to think that his brand was hip. In order to achieve his objective he had a video team produce a two-minute video with high energy music and lots of quick clips of the original Volkswagen Beetle, the Apple Macintosh and Doug Flutie (the former NFL quarterback). There was no voiceover and there were no words, just lots of energy. I was sitting in the audience when my client kicked off his presentation with that video. When the video ended, he walked out on stage and opened with this line: "So what do a weird looking car, a computer, and a 5'11" NFL quarterback have in common?" He gave a dramatic pause and then proclaimed that each one of them was a brand that transcended other brands; they were brands that people really liked, trusted and could identify with. He then showed a photo of his brand and said, "The same is true for our brand, Rolling Rock." It definitely got the crowd jazzed.

If you don't have the budget to pay for a production company, you'll have to be craftier. The good news is that the hand-held camera approach is very popular in commercials and film and therefore can work very well for your purposes. I once saw a video that some employees did that spoofed their department by playing off on the *Star Wars* characters. It was very entertaining and probably cost less than $100 to produce.

By the way, if you don't know about Microsoft's Movie Maker or Apple's iMovie, check them out. They may already be pre-loaded on your computer and they're a simple and fun way to create your own movie. If you go this route, you might try doing what is referred to as a "mockumentary." The winning formula for this type of spoof video is to show (or talk about) absurd situations as if they were perfectly normal. For example:

- *Lifetime Achievement Award...* This is a very funny way to goof on a senior person or someone who is retiring. Go around and interview people who know (or don't know) the person. They all give off-beat, deadpan answers to seemingly earnest questions such as, "You carpool with Ed. What's it like spending an hour and a half a day in an enclosed box with him?" "You started working with Ed 25 years ago in the mailroom. Did you notice anything special about him then?" "Are you aware of any hobbies Ed has that seem a little peculiar?" "If Ed was a rodent, what kind of rodent would he be?"

- *A Day in the Life of...* The mockumentary takes the

viewer through a typical day in the life of the person featured. Of course it's all a farce. You see the person getting dressed and is stuck on deciding whether to go with the black socks, dark charcoal or midnight slate. Or another scene could be him standing in the cafeteria and having the cashier yell at him for not having exact change. Just before Bill Gates left Microsoft, the company produced a parody video of what his last day of work might look like. It was a hoot. (You can check it out on YouTube.)

• **Words of Wisdom** - A variety of people are interviewed and asked to share their philosophy about what it takes to be a success. The answers they give are either totally confusing, painfully obvious or twisted in some bizarre way. Again, when they give their answer, their delivery should be absolutely deadpan...that's where the laughs will come from. Deadpan, deadpan, deadpan.

Try integrating a short video clip into your presentation, meeting, or sales pitch.

DEMONSTRATIONS

Demos are great. Anytime you can take words and turn them into actions, you'll be more engaging - particularly

if you have a concept or idea that is difficult for people to grasp. For example, in the areas of high tech as well as in the sciences, presenters frequently are called upon to explain some new process or discovery. This is the perfect time to take some three-dimensional objects and transform the conceptual into the concrete.

A few years back, The History Channel aired a program that featured two high school physics teachers who were greatly admired by their students. Besides unbridled enthusiasm for their subject, they always seemed to figure out compelling ways to make dry principles come alive. They'd use brooms, glasses, metal tubes, vacuum cleaners, pillows, books, cars, and rope in order to give their students a hands-on experience. They'd even take their students to amusement parks so the kids could see various physics principals come alive. (These two teachers knew how to hook an audience!)

In my *Breakthrough Thinking* seminar, there's a part in the program where the participants have to figure out a brainteaser that involves getting four explorers across a bridge within a certain amount of time before the proverbial cannibals start munching on them. In order to help participants solve the problem, I asked them to get out of their seats and actually walk through the solution. Besides being a heck of a lot more interactive, the class does a better job solving the problem because they can actually see potential solutions that they couldn't see when they simply talked it over.

My favorite demo is one that I do when I teach conflict resolution. Unbeknownst to the participants, I pre-recruit an audience member to challenge me at some point during the class. When the moment occurs, I act defensive and retaliate. It quickly escalates into a conflict. The onlookers are stunned. After about 20 seconds, I inform the audience that it was all a setup and then we discuss what they just observed. This demo is a showstopper. It's a hundred times more powerful than if I just talked about conflict.

How might you work a demo into your next presentation or meeting?

"*Speak properly, and in as few words as you can, but always plainly; for the end of speech is not ostentation, but to be understood.*"

William Penn

QUIZZES

Another great way to hook an audience is by weaving in some offbeat quizzes, trick questions, or brainteasers into your presentation - especially when you're running a training seminar or a meeting. Quizzes are an excellent way to break the ice and, if facilitated well, can add a buzz to an otherwise humdrum meeting. People like quizzes because they're inter-

> **FINISHED FILES ARE THE RE-SULT OF YEARS OF SCIENTIF-IC STUDY COMBINED WITH THE EXPERIENCE OF YEARS**
>
> How many F's can you find?

active, they're fun and they get a little competition going. And if you blend in some serious questions, they help you know whether or not the audience is retaining important information.

Below is a small sampling of some fun quiz questions. As you'll see, these are all rather general, but with a little re-search, you could easily find, or create, questions that are directly related to your topic, company, competition or coworkers. Your quiz questions can be either open-ended (as seen below) or multiple choice. It all depends on your objective. Lastly, quiz questions can be collected from a variety of sources including quiz books, on-line searches, or from a friend.

Q. Half of all Americans live within 50 miles of what?
A. Their birthplace

Q. Most boat owners name their boats. What is the most popular boat name requested?
A. Obsession

Q. If you were to spell out numbers, how far would you have to go until you would find the letter "A"?
A. One thousand

Q. What is the only food that doesn't spoil?
A. Honey

Q. There are more collect calls on this day than any other day of the year?
A. Father's Day

Q. What is it about Mel Blanc (the voice of Bugs Bunny) that's very ironic?
A. He was allergic to carrots.

Q. What is an activity performed by 40% of all guests at a party?
A. They snoop in the medicine cabinet.

Q. What do bulletproof vests, fire escapes, windshield wipers, and laser printers all have in common?
A. All invented by women.

Q. What occurs more often in December than any
   other month?
A. Conception.

Here's a terrific quiz question my daughter's friend asked
me:

*You have thirty sick sheep and one dies, how many do you
have left?*

The answer, of course, is twenty-nine. However, when I ask
the question aloud, most people interpret it as: "You have
thirty-six sheep and one dies...how many do you have?"
Therefore they're likely to say thirty-five. I ask the question a
few more times until they come up with the right answer or
until they threaten to harm me (whichever comes first). As

the presenter or facilitator, you can draw a few interesting implications from the sheep question. Or, better yet, have your audience come up with their own implications. Here are just three of the many ways that the sheep question could be a springboard to more substantive issues:

- Sometimes people hear what they expect to hear rather than what is actually said.
- We need to break things down into smaller pieces if we truly want to understand a problem.
- If we rush things, we're bound to miss some important details.

Although I have yet to do it this way, it might be interesting to give the sheep question as a handout to half my audience and to the other half read it out loud. I think it's safe to say that the two groups would come up with different answers and therefore the point you could make is: *How* a question is asked can make a big difference in how it is answered.

GIVEAWAYS

Everybody loves a freebee. Let me repeat. Everybody loves a freebee. What can you give out at your next presentation that your audience will appreciate and will help make your message stick?

As I see it, you have a couple of options. You can either give out chachkas to everyone, or you can go for a bigger ticket item and give out just a few. But remember, you want to make certain that your giveaway ties right back to your main message. If it's a giveaway just for the sake of having a giveaway, you're missing an opportunity to drive home your message.

A few years ago I was asked to coach a marketing VP who was preparing to give a presentation to his Board of Directors. Essentially, he was seeking six million dollars to invest in the manufacturing and marketing of thermostats, a new line of business for the company.

After the VP did a dry run for me, I told him what was working well and where I felt his opportunity for improvement was. The biggest issue I had was that there was no hook. There were lots of slides and plenty of data, but no "wow factor." After I shared some examples of what I meant by having a hook, he agreed that his presentation lacked one and he assured me that he was going to come up with an attention grabber.

Two weeks after the coaching session I received a phone call from the VP and he started the conversation by saying, "The Board couldn't give me the money fast enough." He then went on to explain how he hooked them:

> *I started off by holding up an iPod nano and I said, "The iPod is the most popular music player available today. Since appearing in 2001, nothing has been able to surpass it. The iPod brings so much to the table. It has added millions to the bottom line and it has put Apple back on the map as a technology leader." I then paused, looked directly at everyone and said, "Ladies and gentleman...we have the opportunity to create our own iPod...we have an idea that will get us into more accounts, will boost our distribution, will provide higher margins and will give us a whole lot of PR." I reached under the table, held up a thermostat and simply said "I'm talking about thermostatic controls." I then told the board, "The first person who can tell me what "RRR" stands for in my presentation will win the iPod nano that I have in front of me." I then started my PowerPoint presentation. About 20 min-*

utes into my pitch, one of the board members raised his hand and gave the answer to my RRR question. When I awarded him his prize the other Board Members, believe it or not, looked jealous. I knew that I had hooked them all. At the end of my presentation I told everyone that I actually had iPods for everyone in the room, but that the gift came with a stipulation and that stipulation was that anytime they looked at their iPod, picked up their iPod or listened to their iPod, they had to think...thermostatic controls!

Now some of our more literal readers may be thinking "Yeah, right, I'm supposed to give out iPods everytime I give a presentation." No, not at all. You could give out almost anything as long as it ties into your message and has some perceived value. If you're talking about transformation, for example, you could plug in a microwave oven, pop some popcorn (in front of everyone) and transform the kernels into popcorn and then give everybody a bag on their way out. I guarantee they'll remember your message. Other giveaways such as books, DVDs, t-shirts (customized with your message, of course) can work great.

By the way, when I'm consulting with my clients, they sometimes say to me "But what I talk about is so boring, there's nothing I can do to make it interesting." I tell them the above story. If thermostats can sound exciting, then pretty much anything can sound exciting.

GAMES AND INTERACTIVITY

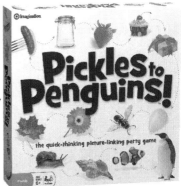

I love games. Board games, improv games, card games...you name it. Games are great because they engage people, they're fun and they can be used to deliver a message. In fact, some companies have hired me for the sole purpose of weaving in a variety of games and interactive exercises throughout their one or two-day meeting in order to keep the audience involved and to help reinforce the theme of their meeting whether it be about leadership, change, teamwork or what have you. Over the years I've collected or created more than 100 activities (aka, games) which I pick and choose from as needed.

As with all hooks, when you integrate games into your message you want to find ones that are fun, easy to facilitate, and tie directly into the point(s) you're making.

Here's a brief overview of three games that I've used many times over the years. You're welcome to try these or, better yet, start collecting your own favorites. There are plenty of resources available to help you find games. Do a Google search on "training games" and you're sure to come up with lots of options.

The Ad Agency Game

This game is fabulous! I use it to teach a variety of lessons such as staying positive, supporting your team, creativity, adaptability and presentation skills. The game is perfect for any group with 15 to 35 people.

Here's how the game works:

Break the audience into teams with four to six people on each team. Teams are then given 15 minutes to come up with a name, slogan, celebrity spokesperson, jingle and TV commercial for a new type of dog food that, when your dog eats it, he can talk! Pretty amazing stuff. (Rather than the dog food, you can assign the teams any crazy, newfan-

gled product or service you'd like.) After the time is up, I give them five more minutes to pull their presentations together so they're prepared to deliver it in front of the entire group.

Now here's the kicker...right before the teams start brain-storming, I tell them that the team must enthusiastically ac-cept (which means scream and yell) whatever ideas their teammates come up with. They are not allowed to sit quietly and ponder. This positive energy gets the room rocking.

After the presentations are over I lead a discussion based on some of the issues I mentioned above (teamwork, presentation skills, etc).

Count

This works well with groups from 10 to 100.

Start by breaking the large group into smaller groups with about 10 to 15 people in each. (They can be sitting or standing.) Tell them that no one is allowed to speak. The object is for the group to count from 1 to 15 given these constraints:

- Only one person may speak at a time. If more than one person speaks (i.e.two people say a number at the same time), then the group must start over.
- There can't be a pattern. In other words, they can't go around in a circle saying numbers. It has to be random. No one knows who will speak next.
- Participants can say more than one number during the game, but they can't say more than one number at a time.
- If the group accomplishes the task, I sometimes have them do it again, but this time with their eyes closed!

I use this game to facilitate discussions about listening, teamwork, problem solving, patience and more.

Point North

This is a quickie that can work with very large and very small groups.

Have everyone in the audience stand up and close their eyes. Then say, "With your eyes closed, I want you to take a moment and try to figure out where North is. Once you think you have it figured out, I want you to point in that direction while still keeping you eyes closed.

Once everyone has pointed, I have them open their eyes. Obviously, people will be pointing in all sorts of directions which usually gets a good laugh.

This exercise is an excellent segue into a variety of issues including:

- We all need to be on the same page before we start a new project.
- Different people have different ways of accomplishing the same task.
- There are lots of opinions, but sometimes there's only one right answer.
- No matter what job you're doing, make sure you have the right tools.
- It's important to be observant of the world around you.

A variation on this game could be to allow the participants to do it with their eyes open and see how some people are influenced by other people. You could even try it with eyes closed and then without eyes closed and see if people changed their opinion and why. Additionally, it might be interesting in a smaller group to see if a group consensus can be arrived at and how it was (or was not) achieved. No matter which way you play it, be sure to bring a compass.

QUOTES

I don't get all that excited about using other people's quotes in my presentations. Not that there's anything wrong with them, in fact, I often use them in my books. It's just that in presentations I don't think quotes pack much punch. As far as I'm concerned, if you're trying to juice up your presentations and meetings, quotes are the bare minimum. With that said, there are things you can do to help make quotes more impactful:

- Find quotes that have an emotional hook.
- Find funny quotes.
- Use mock quotes. (These are a riot).
- Leave out a key word or the author's name and have your audience try and guess the answer. (This creates interaction which is good.)

Here are a handful of quotes from the inspiring to the inane. Go to www.quotationspage.com and you'll find a ton more. Look for quotes that are punchy and powerful. Humdrum quotes just don't cut it.

"Knowledge is Power."

Never interrupt your enemy when he's making a mistake. -- Napoleon

What counts is not necessarily the size of the dog in the fight; it's the size of the fight in the dog.
                                            -- Dwight Eisenhower

Management is doing things right; leadership is doing the right things. -- Peter Drucker

Divide and conquer. -- Julius Caesar

Inches make champions. -- Vince Lombardi

The only thing worse than watching a bad movie is being in one. -- Elvis Presley

This is the most exciting thing I've seen since Halley's Comet collided with the moon. -- Homer (Simpson)

I often reference Steve Jobs in my workshops because I think he's a terrific presenter. He's confident, he speaks with passion, he keeps his message simple, his slides are big, bold and uncluttered, and he says some pretty smart things. Find someone you admire and work some of his or her quotes into your presentation. Here are a bunch of Steve Jobs quotes. I found these in an article by Simran Khurana on About.com

On strategy:

Innovation has nothing to do with how many R&D dollars you have. When Apple came up with the Mac, IBM was spending at least 100 times more on R&D. It's not about money. It's about the people you have, how you're led, and how much you get it.

It's really hard to design products by focus groups. A lot of times people don't know what they want until you show it to them.

It comes from saying no to 1,000 things to make sure we don't get on the wrong track or try to do too much.

Nobody has tried to swallow us since I've been here. I think they are afraid how we would taste.

I once found a bunch of mock quotes online and weaved them in with bona fide inspirational quotes during a client meeting. I started with the real quotes and then introduced the bogus quotes. The audience loved it. Here are a few of my favorite mock quotes:

- *A day without sunshine is like, well, night.*
- *On the other hand, you have different fingers.*
- *Change is inevitable, except from a vending machine.*
- *I just got lost in thought. It was unfamiliar territory.*
- *When the chips are down, the buffalo is empty.*

- *Seen it all, done it all, can't remember most of it.*
- *The beatings will continue until morale improves.*
- *I feel like I'm diagonally parked in a parallel universe.*

Try this. Weave some of the above quotes into your next big presentation and attribute each quote to someone different in the audience. it will get a big laugh from the crowd. (On the other hand, you might get fired, so think about it carefully.)

"Curiosity is the key to creativity."

———————————————————————————

Aiko Morita

SLOGANS & TAGLINES

A little dab'll do ya!

In ten words or less, can you come up with a catchy line that captures the essence of your presentation? If you can, then you have yourself a slogan or what others might call a tagline, motto, sound bite or theme line. Slogans and taglines are different from quotes. Slogans and taglines come from you. Quotes are borrowed from someone else.

Slogans are a fantastic way to help your audience remember your key message because slogans are usually brief and witty, thus making them memorable. While it's true that most day-to-day presentations don't need a tagline, important presentations and speeches should have one. Your goal should be to find a powerful line that becomes the essence of what you're saying. I've heard it referred to as "the phrase that pays."

Arguably, the most famous line from a speech in modern times is "I have a dream." Here it is, over fifty years later and those four words still resonate. Clearly, Martin Luther King found a theme line that worked! How about Gordon

Gekko the character from the classic film *Wall Street?* Remember his slogan? *Greed is good.* And Simon Cowell, from *American Idol* fame, once told a contestant who had had a strong comeback after a bad performance the week before: "You've gone from zero to hero."

But what about yourself? Can you come up with a slogan or tagline that's so good that others will be quoting *you?*

Here are a few examples of where I've seen taglines used to great effect in important speeches, presentations and pieces of communication:

- A CEO wanted his employees to be more mindful of the importance of maintaining positive cash flow through better managing inventory, accounts receivables and accounts payables. In order to get his message to stick with the employees, his communications team came up with the tagline: "Got Cash?" and they married the slogan to a picture of the CEO who had a green milk mustache.

- A good friend of mine recently received an outstanding achievement award from The Boys and Girls Club and had to give a short speech. The theme line he used throughout his presentation was "Together, we can turn fear into hope."

- President Reagan, on June 12, 1987, while standing along side the Berlin Wall that divided East and West German sectors said, "Mr. Gorbachev, tear down this wall!". It fell in 1989.

- And speaking of the Reagans, Nancy Reagan's anti-drug campaign had a very memorable three word theme line: "Just say no."

Can you recall what products go with these classic tag-lines? (The older you are, the better you'll do.)

- Just Do It.
- We try harder.
- Be all you can be.
- Diamonds are forever.
- Snap, Crackle, Pop
- It's the real thing.
- All the news that's fit to print.
- Don't leave home without it.
- Good to the last drop.
- Finger-lickin' good.

The next time you have an important speech, presentation, or sales pitch to give, think about how you can condense your message into one captivating, short tagline. If it'll work on a billboard, it'll work in your pitch.

CARTOONS

Plenty of businesspeople and teachers integrate cartoons into their presentations as a way to add fun into their content. Cartoons are a nice little device that you can use to get a smile from the crowd, but people probably won't come running out of the meeting room saying, "Did you see that hilarious cartoon he projected on the screen?" It's more like getting a peck on the cheek from your Aunt Joan in Cleveland....pleasant, but after it was over you wouldn't go around telling people about it. (That was an analogy, by the way.)

Now don't get me wrong, I'm not against using cartoons, it's certainly a lot better than having nothing, but there are a few reasons why they're not high on my list of hooks. First, there's nothing all that surprising about having a cartoon in a presentation; it's done quite frequently. Second, cartoons are sometimes difficult to read when projected onto a screen. And third, people read and process information at different speeds, so you usually end up getting a soft ripple of "tee-hee's" rather than one big belly laugh.

Just because they're not my favorite, doesn't mean you shouldn't try using cartoons. Cartoonbank.com is a terrific resource.

An alternative to cartoons would be to find some photographs that are visually funny the instant you see them. This way, you're not relying on your audience to read anything. So no matter if you're talking about a new production process, improving plant safety, taking risk, or managing customer expectations, you can easily find some humorous photos that could work well. Here are three funny photos I came across while surfing the internet. I've created a sample gag line for each one to show you how easy it would be to integrate photos like these into any presentation:

"A rare baby photo of Tom Reynolds, our new Transportation Director"

"We recently hired a consultant to help with our sales forcast"

"Our Ethics Review Board"

HODGEPODGE

I've covered all the major hooks in detail, but there's more. Here's a brief assortment of other hooks that I'd recommend you consider.

Initials

Try creating a collection of *memorable* initials that you can weave into your content. Since I frequently have to give presentations on how to sell effectively, rather than talking about the topic in generic (i.e., forgettable) terms, I packaged my presentation as: *Navigating the Sale with GPS.* I created a three-step selling process where the G stands for "Gather information" P stands for "Provide direction" and S stands for "Sell a specific solution." The letters GPS become a simple and memorable way to communicate my selling process.

Similarly, a client of mine once had to give an important presentation where he wanted to share his design philosophy with a group of potential clients. We needed to find a hook  whereby he could communicate his whole approach in a matter of minutes. We came up with four very memorable letters **(WXYZ)** that he built his philosophy around.

- **W** stood for "**W**hat if possibilities...?"
- **X** stood for "e**X**amine your brand essence"
- **Y** stood for "**Y**our put-up-withs"
- **Z** stood for the name of his company, which started with the letter **Z**.

My client delivered an awesome seven-minute presentation working off just a handful of slides. If you go to the *Testimonials* page on my website you'll hear a brief voicemail he left me after his pitch. This will give you a sense of the type of result you'll get when you find a great hook.

The last example of the effective use of initials was when a radio reporter was covering the story of AIG, the disgraced financial giant. He said, "Nowadays AIG stands for Arrogance, Incompetence and Greed."

Acronyms

The other option with letters is to create an acronym. Here's a list of acronyms that are used in various industries in various parts of the world. A number of the terms have a fun twist to them, so you can see how acronyms can make ideas stick. What acronyms can you come up with that have to do with your line of work and that you could integrate into your next meeting?

DINKY: *Double Income No Kids Yet*
GLAM: *Greying, Leisured, Affluent, Married.*

DIN: *Do It Now*
HEW: *High Earning Worker*
ERIC: *Emotional Reaction Impedes Control*
NINJA: *No Income, No Job or Assets*
FIFO: *First In First Out*
FORCE: *Focus On Reducing Costs Everywhere*
HIP: *High Involvement Product*
ITALY: *I Trust And Love You*
PICNIC: *Problem In Chair, Not In Computer*
FIGS: *French, Italian, German, Spanish*
KEV: *Key Ethical Value*
RICE: *Rest, Ice, Compression, Elevation*
BURP: *Bankrupt Unemployed Rejected Person*
YOYO: *You're On Your Own*

G.A.R.G.L.E.

A Mnemonic Sentence

One time a speaker gave a presentation to an audience of financial planners where he was talking about Robert Cialdini's seven forces of persuasion. (They are: self interest, reciprocity, social proof, authority, likeability, scarcity, and continuity.) In order to help the audience remember the list, the speaker came up with this mnemonic sentence: *Ships Returning Slowly, Always Land Safe Cargo*. The first letter of each word in the sentence corresponded with the first letter in each item on Cialdini's list. And if that mnemonic sentence wasn't memorable enough, during the break the speaker challenged his audience to come up with their own mnemonic sentence using those same seven letters, but related to financial services.

Music

Here are three examples of how music has been used in presentations:

1. A facilitator kicks off her empowerment workshops by playing Aretha Franklin's *Respect*.
2. A sales manager blasts Booker T and the MGs to get his audience energized.
3. A communication teacher plays two different versions of *Mary Had a Little Lamb* to show how the same words can have an entirely different meaning depending on how they're delivered. One version is sung by the Wiggleworms, a kiddy band, and the other by Stevie Ray Vaughn, a blues singer.

Music moves people, music motivates people, and music helps people remember. How might you work music into a meeting or presentation? Keep in mind that there are certain rules and regulations as to when and where you can play commercial music in public. To find out more, go to www.ascap.com.

Sound Effects

A software marketer planned to kick off his brand presentation with a story about how much he loved to ride his Harley Davidson (which, of course, he was going to connect directly to the main point in his presentation, as I have been saying over and over.) We had discussed the possibility of having him ride in on a Harley, but given all the logistics, safety issues, cost and insurance concerns, we needed to come up with a different grabber. The solution was simple and striking. Right after the brand manager was introduced, but before he walked on stage, we blasted an awesome sound effect of a Harley starting up and driving off. When the brand manager came out with his leather jacket on, he had the attention of hundreds of salespeople instantly.

I-Mag (Image Magnification)

In big meetings the speaker's image is often projected on a huge screen on stage. This device can be an unexpected and creative way to hook an audience. Some years ago we rigged up a pretend "satellite feed" so that the speaker on stage could talk live to some of her marketing people "around the world." The hook was that her people weren't around the world at all; they were backstage standing in front of some campy backdrops of Big Ben, an Oktoberfest beer hall and things like that. The audience knew it was all a joke and enjoyed the tongue-in-cheek gag. If you've ever seen *The Daily Show* with Jon Stewart, you'll see this technique used all the time.

Top Ten List

Made famous by David Letterman, the Top Ten List is relatively easy to do and is a great icebreaker. You can make this concept work for pretty much any topic. For example, I had a friend who decided to hold his sales meeting in Buffalo in January. Knowing that he was going to get some flack from the attendees, he opened the meeting with **The Top Ten Reasons We Decided to Hold Our Meeting in Buffalo in January.** It was an easy way to get everybody laughing and to poke some good-natured fun at himself. (By the way, audiences love it when speakers take a fun shot at themselves.)

Magic

I could probably do a whole chapter on magic and how to work it in to a presentation, but since I'm a lousy magician, I won't go there. A friend of mine, however, *is* a great magician and is a professional speaker, too. He integrates magic into his speeches all the time. If you know a couple of magic tricks, or are willing to learn a few (visit YouTube for this), magic can be woven into your presentation to grab attention and reinforce your message. Here are a few examples:

• The topic: Change. The trick: Turn a cane into a bouquet of flowers

- The topic: Finance. The trick: Make a coin disappear
- The topic: Succession planning. The trick: Saw the CEO in half!

Skits

I've seen live skits where the employees/presenters get up in front of the room (particularly at a national sales meeting or annual offsite where fun is part of the agenda) and act out various scenes such as a customer service interaction or a safety incident. Most often the skits are spoofs, but they don't have to be. Some years ago a school bus company gave each department the challenge of coming up with a scene that best communicated the company's mission statement. The audience got to vote on the best skit and awards were given. It was a unique and interactive way to get the employees to examine the company's strategic direction and what it meant to them.

Be cautious. I've seen skits slapped together at the last minutes and they were pretty lame. With a little preplanning, skits can be a fun and creative way to get lots of people involved in communicating your message.

Historical Events...*This day in history*

With a little web research you can come up with some interesting tidbits on notable events that happened way back when. For example: On this day in 1962, John Glenn was the first American to orbit the earth...and today we are the first American company to _____.

"I look at what the phone company does and do the opposite."

Craig Newmark

BONUS ROUND

If you ever want to bring down the house, let's say at a national sales meeting, kickoff event, or a holiday party, one of the best ways to do this is by roasting your audience. Audiences love to laugh and they love to laugh at themselves. In fact roasts are so much fun that I've been doing them for my clients for over 20 years. Below I've shared with you my two most popular roast concepts. If you have some proficiency with Adobe Photoshop, you'll be able to produce your own. (But then again, you can always call me.)

Roast Concept # 1 - Phony Magazine Covers

With this concept, you need to get inside information on the person (or people) to be roasted. You'll want to know things about their personality, job responsibilities, favorite sayings, trivia and so forth. Once you get the lowdown, you then create hilarious magazine covers featuring the roastees. When it's all said and done, you end up with a slide show and script that runs about 15 to 20 minutes and brings down the house every time. Here are a few sample covers I've created in the past.

Roast Concept # 2 - Genetic Reengineering

The other roast that's a sure winner is *Genetic Reengineering.* What you do here is take the headshots of two employees and make them into one. The result is too funny for words. You'll want photos of about 20 to 30 people and from those you can make 10 to 15 combinations. Then you'll want to come up with new names, personality quirks and job responsibilities for the clone combos. This concept is a killer.

If you go to www.kevincarrollcomedy.com, you'll be able to see a video clip of a roast I did a number of years ago.

KEY TAKEAWAYS

1. Start a "Keeper" file so you can begin collecting all sorts of interesting hooks that you'll be able to work into your presentations, meetings, and conversations.

2. Make certain that your message has relevancy and value for your listener, otherwise, why would they care? This is particularly important on job interviews and sales calls.

3. State your points clearly and concisely so that an eight-grader would be able to understand you.

4. Organize your presentation so that it's easy for both you and your listener to track through it. My book, *Make Your Point!*, will help you with this.

5. Speak with a healthy dose of energy and enthusiasm. Project your voice so that the people in the back of the room can easily hear you.

6. Avoid jargon such as: "We need to recalibrate our commitment to the simplification initiative."

7. Watch out for TMI (too much information). It bores and confuses audiences. This applies to emails, too.

8. When giving a presentation, have a minimal number of slides, with minimal information on each slide.

9. Make your slides visually interesting by incorporating pictures and photographs.

10. Find ways to get your audience involved. When you ask your listener questions, you create a dialogue versus a monologue.

11. When someone asks a question, be certain you're clear about what they're asking *before* you start answering the question.

12. If you work more hooks into your presentations, meetings, conversations and emails, your ride to the top will be faster and more fun.

ABOUT THE AUTHOR
(Kevin Carroll: A life in bullet points)

• The third of seven kids from a boisterous Irish family.

• Grew up just outside New York City.

• Worked in advertising for 17 years. (Got out on account of good behavior.)

• Once tried stand-up comedy. (His career was described as "short and dubious.")

• In 1996 started his own corporate training business. His motto: *Think Creatively. Communicate Persuasively.*

• Most memorable assignment: teaching conflict resolution at the US Postal Service. (Seriously.)

• Clients have included: Microsoft, GE, Chubb, Wrigley, Unilever, IBM, and Coleytown Elementary School.

• Written three books: *Make Your Point!, Think Outside Your Blocks, and What's Your Hook?*

• In 2008, created a family board game (with the help of his daughter and a friend of his) called *Pickles to Penguins.*

• Married, two kids, one dog, and lives in Connecticut.

DEDICATION

For the last 25 years I've been trying to figure out what makes a great presenter and how to become a better one myself. The catalyst for this occurred in 1982 when I gave a speech to the Louisville Ad Club. After it was over the audience lined up to tell me how bad it was. I knew then that I had some work to do.

This book is dedicated to everyone who, during the course of their workweek, has to stand up in front of others and communicate their ideas. I'm a firm believer that the ability to be an outstanding communicator is a skill you can develop more than it is an innate talent. If you're willing to break it down, study it and work at it, you can learn how to manage your anxiety, communicate your ideas clearly, engage your audience with hooks, and present with confidence.

Enjoy the trip.

NEXT STEPS

Enjoyed the book? You're invited to share your comments on Amazon.com. All you have to do is search: *What's Your Hook?* Once you see the book, click on it and then click on "Customer Reviews." There you will be able to "Create your own review." Many thanks.

Free excerpts from my other books can be downloaded at: www.kevincarroll.com.

Interested in having me speak at an upcoming event or train your people? Contact me directly:
1. Email: kevin@kevincarroll.com
2. Phone: 1-203-226-6493
3. Website: www.kevincarroll.com
4. Carrier Pigeon: 2 Broad Street - Westport, CT 06880

84229349R00073

Made in the USA
San Bernardino, CA
06 August 2018